Rosa Parks made history on De
her seat on a segregated bus to
The Henry Ford announced tha
would soon be put on display. V

Rosa Parks sparked the American civil rights

anyone be sure? This is the story of how our team of curators and con-
servation specialists decided that this really was the Rosa Parks Bus.

Mrs. Parks' courageous act inspired Montgomery's African-American community to boycott (refuse to ride) the city buses. The boycott was the first successful mass protest mounted by African Americans and brought worldwide attention to the civil rights movement. The boycott was organized by the Montgomery Improvement Association, a group led by a 26-year-old Baptist minister named Martin Luther King, Jr. His powerful speeches and skillful management of the boycott propelled him to national fame as a civil rights leader.

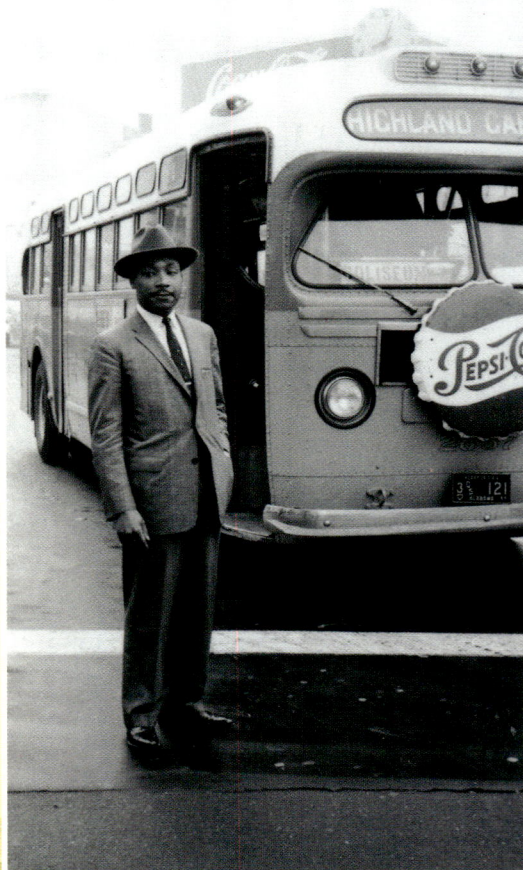

Photo by Don Cravens,
Time-Life Pictures/
Getty Images

Many blacks in Montgomery depended on the bus every day to get them to work, to stores, or to school. Even though refusing to ride was a great hardship, blacks all over the city formed car pools, rode bicycles, or simply walked to avoid riding the bus. Buses across town drove their routes empty. The Montgomery City Lines lost thousands of dollars in revenue during the 381-day boycott.

Photo by Don Cravens, Time-Life Pictures/Getty Images

What happened to the bus after the boycott ended? It continued to be used until 1971 and was retired. However, the bus company did not want to draw attention to Montgomery's history of segregation and the struggle for civil rights, and so made no plans to keep the bus. The bus was sold to Charles Summerford who parked it in a field near Montgomery and used it to store tools and lumber.

Mr. Summerford had been told by bus company employees that this vehicle was the Rosa Parks Bus, and he took pride in telling others about the historic bus he had purchased. But how could *we* tell this bus apart from all the other Montgomery City Lines buses? The 1950s business records of the bus company would be of no help because they were destroyed in the 1970s.

Could we prove that this bus was even in Montgomery in 1955? The bus serial number gave us a clue. Inside the bus we found the original metal identification plate (shown below) that had been installed when the bus was built in 1948. This bus left the factory as coach #1132. When it was purchased by Chicago's National City Lines bus company, it was given a fleet number: 2857. This number was painted on the outside of the bus and above the driver's seat.

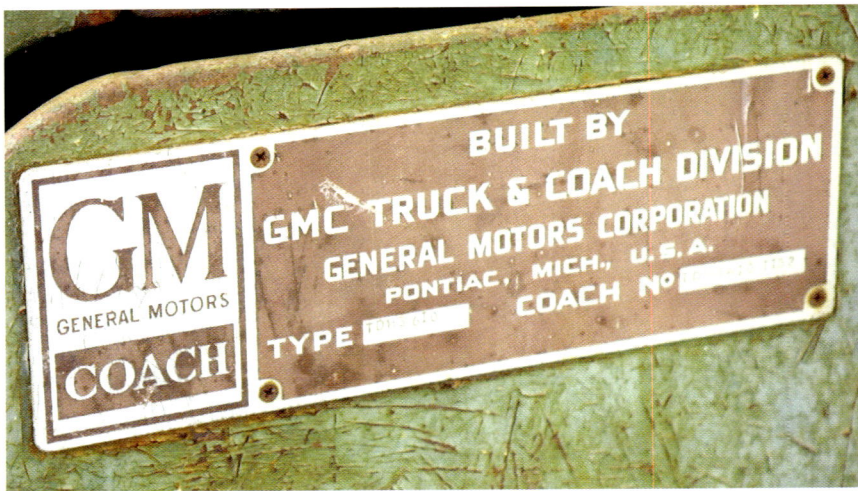

Records revealed that bus #2857 was first sent to Terre Haute, Indiana. Then in 1954, National City Lines sent the bus from Terre Haute to Montgomery, Alabama where it remained in service until 1971. With this information, we had proof that this bus was in Montgomery in 1955.

Could we find any evidence that this was *the* bus on which Mrs. Parks was arrested? The actual fleet number of the bus had not been recorded in photographs, newspaper accounts, or police records back in 1955. In 2001, researchers discovered a scrapbook put together for the Montgomery City Lines in the 1950s. Full of clippings about the boycott, the scrapbook also contained hand-written notations by Charles Homer Cummings (pictured below) who had worked as a manager for the bus company from the 1950s until his death in 1974. He recognized the importance of the boycott and it was his notes that provided the link between Mrs. Parks and this particular bus.

Inside the scrapbook, Mr. Cummings had written "2857" and "Blake/2857" next to newspaper clippings about Mrs. Parks' arrest. These notes indicated the fleet number of the bus on which she was riding, and the name of the driver (James F. Blake). The scrapbook evidence was very convincing, but was it authentic? A forgery expert examined each page of the scrapbook – the newspaper articles, the hand-written notes, even the age of the tape used to hold the clippings in place – and determined that the scrapbook was genuine.

Montgomery Bus Arrest May Bring Test Of Segregation

MONTGOMERY, Ala., Dec. 5.—(AP)—The arrest of a Negro who refused to move to the colored section of a city bus may bring a court test of segregated transportation in the cradle of the Confederacy.

While thousands of other Negroes boycotted Montgomery city lines in protest, Rosa Parks was fined $14 in police court today for disregarding a driver's order to move to the rear of a bus last Thursday.

Negro passengers ride in the rear of the buses here; white passengers in front under a municipal segregation ordinance.

Along with the bus boycott, there were other threatened acts of retaliation by Negroes. A mass meeting was scheduled tonight at a Negro church to consider "further instructions."

The boycott was organized after circulars were distributed in Negro residential areas Saturday urging "economic reprisal" against the bus company.

Released On Bond

The Parks woman appealed her $14 fine and was released under $100 bond signed by Negro Atty. Fred Gray and a former state president of the National Association for the Advancement of Colored People, E. D. Nixon.

Negroes by the thousands found other means of transportation or stayed home today in an organized boycott of city lines buses, operated by a subsidiary of National City Lines at Chicago.

Manager J. H. Bagley estimated that "80 or maybe 90 per cent" of the Negroes who normally use the buses joined the boycott. He said "several thousand" members of the race ride the buses on a normal day.

Police and bus lines officials rode in cars along many of the bus routes to prevent violence after Police Commissioner Clyde Sellers said he had reports some Negroes had been threatened with harm if they took buses to work.

One Negro was arrested on a disorderly conduct charge after officers said he tried to forcibly prevent a Negro woman from boarding a bus.

Blake/#2857

09

Remember fleet #2857? After sitting in a field for thirty years, much of the bus' original paint and markings had worn away. Hunters had shot holes in some of the windows. However, the fleet number was still visible in several places on the bus when we examined it in 2001. Can you find #2857 in these photos?

After reviewing all the evidence, The Henry Ford concluded that bus #2857 was the Rosa Parks Bus.

How did bus #2857 look in 1955? We examined the bus closely, looked at similar buses in other museums, interviewed people who had participated in the boycott, and even found this postcard that showed city buses in downtown Montgomery in the 1950s. This research gave us information about paint colors, seat covers, and other details necessary to make the bus look like it did in 1955.

It took nearly four months to restore the Rosa Parks Bus. The restoration work was performed by MSX Corporation of Auburn Hills, Michigan.

September 2002: Restoration specialists work on repairing the badly rusted body of the Rosa Parks Bus.

October 2002: After the bus was blasted with tiny glass beads and covered with primer paint, workmen spent many hours sanding around hundreds of individual rivets by hand.

Photos by J. Kyle Keener,
Chief Photographer, *Detroit Free Press*.

December 2002: Masking tape is removed after the bus is painted in its original colors.

January 2003: The fully renovated bus, complete with its Montgomery City Lines markings and fleet number, is washed before being put on display at Henry Ford Museum.

Some people have asked why we spent so much time and effort to restore an old bus. Bus #2857 is a common, unremarkable object on which a very remarkable event occurred. It is evidence that the courage and conviction of one person can change history. It is also a reminder that maintaining our freedom and fairness requires our attention every day.

The Rosa Parks Bus is also a symbol – a symbol of the civil rights movement, of the quest for human liberty, and of personal courage and social commitment. The restored bus serves as a tool to help teach the values and legacy of Rosa Parks and the Montgomery Bus Boycott.

Photo by John F. Martin, AP/Wide World Photos

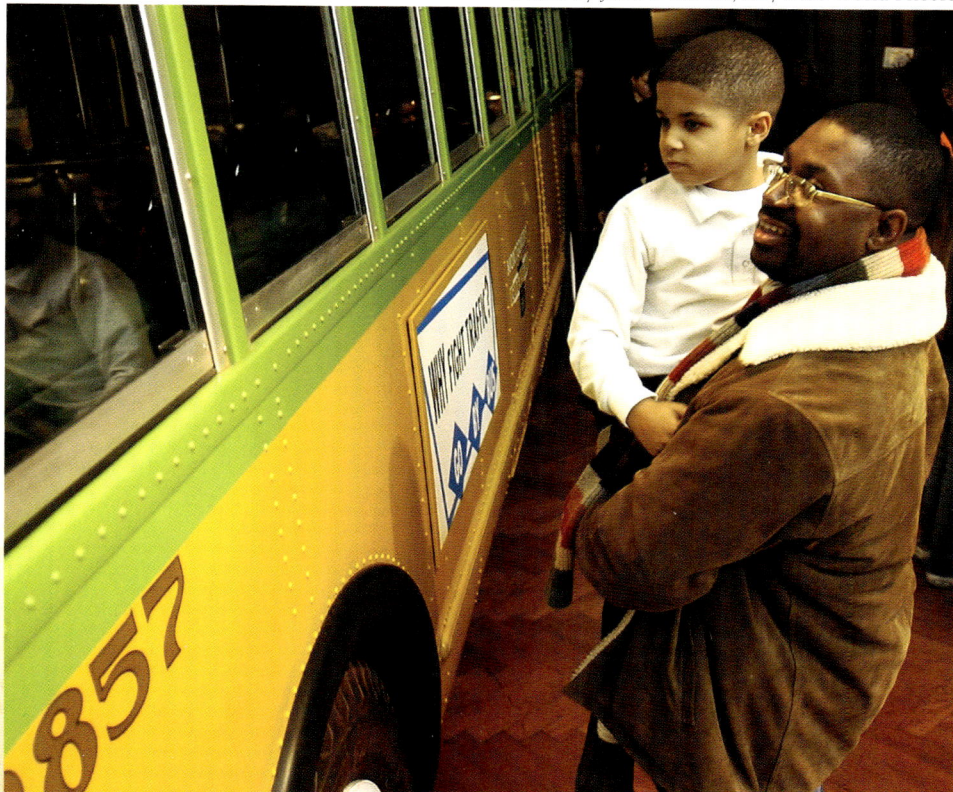

This photograph of Rosa Parks on a Montgomery City Lines bus was taken on December 21, 1956, the day all Montgomery buses were ordered Integrated by the U.S. Supreme Court. Mrs. Parks calls this her "historical honor badge" because it has become one of the most famous photographs in the world, symbolizing the never-ending struggle for human liberty.